Praise for *Changemaker*

"Grassroots advocates pushing for legislative change often feel like David facing off against Goliath. For my fellow Davids, I highly recommend *Changemaker* by veteran labor lobbyist Kristina Bas Hamilton. An inside and practical take on how workers can win legislative campaigns, *Changemaker* boldly recognizes an unsavory truth: the legislative process is far too removed and intimidating for the vast majority of Californians. This means successful advocacy is elusive to those who need it the most. The book aspires to change this by demystifying the legislative process to make it more transparent and accessible. Its powerful message reinforces the idea that, at its core, the best advocacy is led by those who understand the real-life impact of policies, an insight that has the potential to transform the way we engage with our governing institutions."

– Kimberly Alvarenga, Director, California Domestic Workers Coalition

"Thank goodness an advocate as effective as Kristina has taken the time to explain and demystify a complex and nuanced process. This insider's guide will help progressive advocates accelerate their agendas in Sacramento."

– Jennifer Fearing, President, Fearless Advocacy

"*Changemaker* spells out the recipe for success inside California's Capitol: it's the right mix of good planning, building strong relationships, empowering grassroots leaders, and keeping the faith that makes for an effective advocate. The Economic Security Project has partnered with Kristina Bas Hamilton to spearhead legislative strategy to put money directly in the pockets of Californians. Her life's work has made a tangible difference in the lives of many. I hope this book finds its way to the next generation of young leaders who can continue the tough and necessary work of advocating for big, bold ideas through the state legislature."

– Natalie Foster, President and Co-Founder of Economic Security Project and author of *The Guarantee* (April 2024)

"*Changemaker* is an excellent resource for advocates seeking to improve their legislative chops. Easy to digest, it offers invaluable tips and actionable advice on how to build relationships and navigate a notoriously complex legislative process. I highly recommend it for novice and veteran advocates alike."

- Doug Moore, Executive Director, United Domestic Workers/AFSCME Local 3930

"Understanding how to navigate the legislative process is essential for those of us working for justice in California. The process is ripe with opportunities for impacted community members to become active leaders. Kristina Bas Hamilton strikes at the core of this activism with this amazing and powerful book. Every advocate, activist, or community member involved in policy efforts and campaigns should have this book in their toolkit."

– Victor Narro, UCLA Professor, Author, and Activist

"Not since my childhood days of School House Rock have I enjoyed such a clear, concise, and accessible explanation of the legislative process. Kristina Bas Hamilton is proof that "lobbying" need not be a dirty word and that there are good guys — and gals — out fighting the good fight for workers and progressive causes in our halls of power. Advocates everywhere should commend Kristina's generosity in sharing 13 years of hard-won insider knowledge so others can win legislative victories without having to retain paid lobbyists such as herself. Her passion for equity and justice shines through every helpful page."

– Libby Schaaf, 50th Mayor of Oakland and Lecturer at the Goldman School of Public Policy, UC Berkeley

"*Changemaker* is the guidebook all lobbyists wish they had when first starting out. Kristina Bas Hamilton has created a unique and masterful compilation of the "do's and don'ts" of the California legislative process that will not only save advocates time and heartache but will set them up for success. Influencing public policy in the world's fifth-largest economy is a herculean task. *Changemaker* decodes an intricate and often overwhelming process into digestible, actionable steps, making it an invaluable resource for aspiring changemakers. Kristina has done an excellent job reminding us that legislative advocacy isn't just the purview of high-priced professionals but is a tool for everyday Californians to make positive change in their communities."

– Angie Wei, former Legislative Affairs Secretary, Office of Governor Gavin Newsom and former Chief of Staff, California Labor Federation

"Kristina Bas Hamilton is a fierce and indefatigable advocate for many Californians that would otherwise not have a voice in the halls of power. Her new book, *Changemaker*, is essential reading for any advocate who wants to impact state public policy. It is an honest and easy to understand guide to the basics of how to navigate the legislative process and pass a law in California."

– Bill Wong, Award-winning political consultant and Amazon best-selling author of *Better to Win*

CHANGE MAKER

AN INSIDER'S GUIDE TO GETTING SH*T DONE AT THE CALIFORNIA CAPITOL

KRISTINA BAS HAMILTON

For L & E and their generation

Contents

Acknowledgements   1

Introduction   2

Chapter 1: Quick Overview of the   4
California Government

Chapter 2: Thinking Through Your   10
Proposal

Chapter 3: Building Support for Your   20
Proposal

Chapter 4: The Legislative Process   26

Chapter 5: Lobbying Your Legislation   33

Parting Words   42

References   43

About the Author   45

Acknowledgements

Foremost, all my love and appreciation for my husband, James Hamilton. My partner in crime and greatest cheerleader. Despite my long days at work and time away from home, his support and patience never once wavered.

Love & Light to my parents and siblings - Bartolome Bas, Anna Bas, Anton Bas, and Natalia Bas Granda.

To the mentors, colleagues, allies, and friends too numerous to count who have given me invaluable guidance and assistance during the ups and downs of my advocacy journey THANK YOU.

I specifically want to thank Doug Moore and my UDW family, Willie Pelote, and Jovan Agee for giving this Jersey girl a chance to spread her wings in California.

Thank you to Abby Alvarez, Andrea Amavisca, Sarah Bouabibsa, Samantha Contreras, Joyce Jang, Lex Roman, Arianna Z. Smith, Aaron Vad, and Bill Wong for lending your unique insight and expertise to this project.

Special shout out to the Blueprint for California Advocates community. Your enthusiasm and energy keep me going.

Finally, I stand in solidarity with workers and allies everywhere fighting to build a more just and equitable world.

Introduction

"We are the ones we have been waiting for."

– June Jordan

When I think back to my time as Legislative Director for the United Domestic Workers, one of the largest and most active unions in California, the memories I cherish most are the days when rank and file union members traveled from around the state to Sacramento to take part in legislative hearings or lobby visits with their state representatives.

For many union members, it was their first time engaging in legislative advocacy. I could sense some trepidation and nervousness as we entered the Capitol building. However, once the workers finished presenting their testimony or meeting with lawmakers, there was a palpable shift in energy. Uncertainty evaporated and was replaced by pride and determination. Workers left empowered and grateful for the experience. This positive transformation never failed to move me. The best part was they couldn't wait to come back.

For most Californians - and Americans - government is something distant and untouchable. I know first-hand though that when working people are plugged into the process, when they have the access and opportunity to engage consistently with lawmakers to speak firsthand about their needs and those of their families and communities, government can change for the better.

This book is a compilation of the tips and tricks I've learned - many the hard way - over thirteen years as a labor lobbyist. I hope that it helps break down barriers, if even in some small way, that have historically kept the institution of government inaccessible to the very people who need it most.

If you're a Californian who wants to make positive change in your community through the legislative process but don't know where to start, I hope this book gives you the confidence you need to step up and get involved. If you've already engaged in legislative campaigns and want to elevate your work, I hope this guide gives you the insight to go bigger and bolder.

I want to see you win.

Chapter 1: Quick Overview of the California Government

To be an effective advocate, you need a good understanding of how the California government works. I've defined legislative terminology throughout this book, but if you want more in depth explanations, you may want to refer to the Glossary published by the Office of Legislative Counsel. The link can be found in the References section of this book, along with other resources.

When people think of the government, they often think of the federal level, like the President and Vice President. But you'll have a better chance of creating change if you stick closer to home – in local communities and at the state level.

Three Branches of California Government

Like our federal government, our state government has three branches: Judicial, Executive, and Legislative.

Judicial Branch

The Judicial branch is made up of the state Supreme Court and lower courts. Their job is to interpret California state law and ensure it is not in conflict with the State Constitution. The Judicial branch does not make laws; instead, it ensures that the laws that are passed are applied equally and justly in cases that appear before the courts.

Executive Branch

The role of the Executive Branch is to execute or carry out California state law. It is led by the Governor. This branch includes all the statewide elected officials and appointed officers. It works closely with the state's Legislative branch to shape the legislation it administers and enforces.

The Executive branch is responsible for three key things related to our purposes here:

- The Governor proposes a state budget to the Legislature in January and again in May of each year.

- The Governor signs or vetoes legislation, including the state budget.

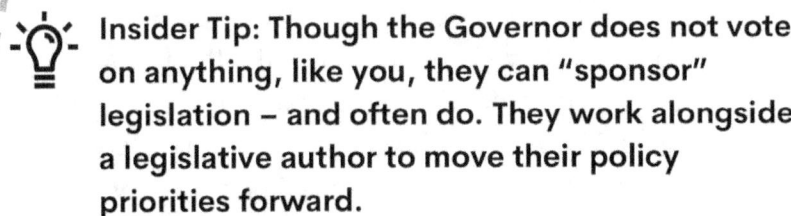

- The Governor makes appointments to key positions in state government as well as the judiciary.

Insider Tip: Though the Governor does not vote on anything, like you, they can "sponsor" legislation – and often do. They work alongside a legislative author to move their policy priorities forward.

It's important to know whom the Governor has appointed to their Cabinet. These are the Secretaries and Directors of major California agencies and departments. You will want to become familiar with the cabinet member(s) responsible for the policy area of your advocacy.

For example, if you are advocating for criminal justice reform, you will want to know who is the head of the Department of Corrections and Rehabilitation. To push for changes to health care policy, you'll need to know the Secretary of Health & Human Services Agency. You get the idea.

There are also elected positions within the Executive branch. Along with the Governor, these are our Constitutional Officers, and they also can play an important role in your advocacy efforts. These include the Lieutenant Governor, State Attorney General, and Secretary of State, among others.

Study the org chart (available online) of the California Executive Branch to learn who's who. In the same way you should know who leads the Agency in charge of your issue area, you'll want to find out which Constitutional Officers have jurisdiction as well.

Legislative Branch

Finally, there's the Legislative branch. Like the federal government, it is bicameral, which means it is comprised of two houses. There's the "upper house" - the State Senate - and the "lower house" – the State Assembly (think of it like the House of Representatives). There are 40 members of the Senate, each of whom represents about 950,000 Californians, and 80 members of the Assembly, each of whom represents about 450,000 Californians. The job of the California Legislature is to make the laws.

In California, the lower house is named the "State Assembly". In other states, it might be named the "House of Representatives", the "House of Delegates", or the "General Assembly".

California is one of only 10 states with a full-time legislature. That makes advocating at the state level for many groups a full-time job. Legislators from all over the state sit in legislative session for eight or nine months out of the year, depending on the year. In comparison, in states with part-time legislatures, lawmakers may meet only a few months of the year or once every other year.

The leader of the State Senate is the Senate President Pro Tempore, referred to as the "Pro Tem" and is elected by a vote of the members of the Senate. The leader of the State Assembly is the Speaker, elected by a vote of the members of the Assembly. Together with the Governor, they are known as the "Big 3".

It's hard to overestimate the power of legislative Leadership. Not much happens in the respective houses of the Pro Tem and Speaker without their blessing. This includes legislative business, such as prioritizing certain bills for approval and appointing individual legislators to certain committees, as well as administrative issues, such as assigning office space to individual legislators and approving raises for legislative staff.

If a legislator is on the "outs" with their respective leader - for doing something like voting against a leader's prioritized bill, for example - they can face retribution such as losing their preferred committee assignments or being re-assigned to the "worst" office spaces. In the old Capitol Annex (now demolished), the smallest, most remote office was known as the "Dog House".

 Insider Tip: When the Assembly Speaker fast-tracks high-priority legislation, we say the bill has been "Speakerized".

Chapter 1 Takeaways

- **OUR THREE BRANCHES:**

The California State Government is comprised of the Judicial branch (the courts), the Executive branch (Governor and State agencies), and the Legislative branch (the State Legislature).

- **WHO, WHAT, AND WHERE?**

It's important to get to know the key decision makers - elected and appointed - in your issue area and what role they play in the process.

- **LEGISLATORS VS LEADERSHIP:**

The Legislature has 120 legislators in 2 separate houses and a powerful legislative leadership that has a big impact on legislative business - including the outcome of individual bills.

Chapter 2: Thinking Through Your Proposal

Now it's time to put pen to paper.

Validating Your Idea

At the heart of every law is an idea to solve a specific problem.

For example, to address a shortage of affordable childcare, you might propose investing more state budget dollars to increase the number of subsidized childcare slots available to low-income families.

There is no scarcity of good ideas, and you likely have several already that you believe would benefit your local community and the state.

It's not enough to like your idea though. You need to robustly vet your proposal to determine whether it has the potential to get signed into law.

Here are some fundamental questions to ask yourself

What - exactly - is the problem we are trying to solve?

This is an obvious first step but bears much repeating. Before you spend time developing your proposal, draft a clear outline of the issue you think needs to be addressed.

What is the scale and scope of what is happening on the ground? Who is it affecting, and why is it a problem? Don't assume lawmakers are already familiar with the issue or problem. In fact, don't assume lawmakers agree with you that it's a problem that needs solving.

Your job is to educate them and make as strong a case as possible. To convince a lawmaker to vote for your legislation, you first need them to agree there is in fact a problem that needs to be addressed.

Is this a federal or local issue?

There are many actions that only Congress or a local government can authorize. You might have a good idea for a law that California as a state has no authority to address.

If the answer to the question above is "yes", don't give up on the idea. Just know that the path to getting a law passed at the federal or local level is very different from getting it passed at the state level, which is the focus of this book.

Do we even need a brand-new law?

It's entirely possible that the law you want to see passed already exists. The problem may be that it's not being implemented or enforced correctly - if at all. Unfortunately, this happens more often than you would think.

So, before you get too far in the process, check local, state, and federal law to see if your idea (or something similar) is already on the books. If it is and the problem is lack of enforcement or bad implementation, then you can turn your advocacy efforts to that.

Is this a legislative or regulatory fix?

 It may be that you don't need a bill because what you want to see happen can be enacted through regulation. Because a bill can't address every detail and scenario that may arise during implementation or enforcement, regulations, or rules, are adopted by state agencies and departments that lay out the nitty-gritty of how laws should work on the ground.

Changing regulations involves a different process entirely and is arguably much easier to accomplish than passing new legislation. Advocating for these changes is called regulatory lobbying.

Are we changing or "amending" an existing law?

This is a big deal because whoever worked to pass the existing law likely will object to you coming along to try and change it. Start by learning the history of current law. When and why was it enacted in the first place? Who led its passage and who opposed it? Have any groups tried to change it in the past? If yes, ask why they failed. Finally, determine who are likely to be your allies and opponents if you move forward.

Insider tip: There may be staff working at the Capitol who were involved in the passage of the original legislation. Ask around - respectfully - and you may be able to find someone who can help you put these puzzle pieces together. However, keep in mind this information is provided as a courtesy. Don't take anything for granted.

Is it Constitutional?

That is, does your proposal violate the terms of the California or US Constitutions? Don't panic if you aren't sure how to answer this question. A good lawyer who specializes in the area of the law you care about can tell you if what you're trying to do will pass muster.

 Insider Tip: if you have the support of a legislator, ask if they can submit on your behalf a formal request to the Office of Legislative Counsel, referred to as "Leg Counsel," to review your proposal and give their legal opinion.

Will it cost the state money to implement the bill?

This is a fundamental question because if the answer is "yes," you almost certainly will also need to advocate for a state budget appropriation to fund your bill. This is a different and separate process from trying to pass a policy bill, and you will have to advocate for both at the same time.

I have seen groups get their legislation all the way to the Governor's desk only to have them issue a veto because the proposal will cost the state millions of dollars to enact, and no funding was set aside in the budget for that purpose. Take time to understand California's budget process and decide if you have the resources to embark on a legislative and budget campaign at the same time.

 Insider Tip: Several episodes of the Blueprint for California Advocates podcast go behind the scenes on the budget process and discuss how budget advocacy really works. You can find them on www.kbhadvocacy.com/podcast or your favorite podcast player.

Start with these fundamental questions before you take the next step of drafting a bill. You don't want to go through the process of writing and proposing a bill only to find out weeks or months later that the bill is not doable for any of the reasons cited above.

Timing and Other Things to Consider

Once you have vetted your idea and settled on what you want to propose, it's time to think about the politics and the logistics involved in running your bill.

Do you have the resources you need to sustain a successful campaign?

You may be proposing the most thoughtful, evidence-based policy in the world, but that alone is often not enough to get a bill past the finish line.

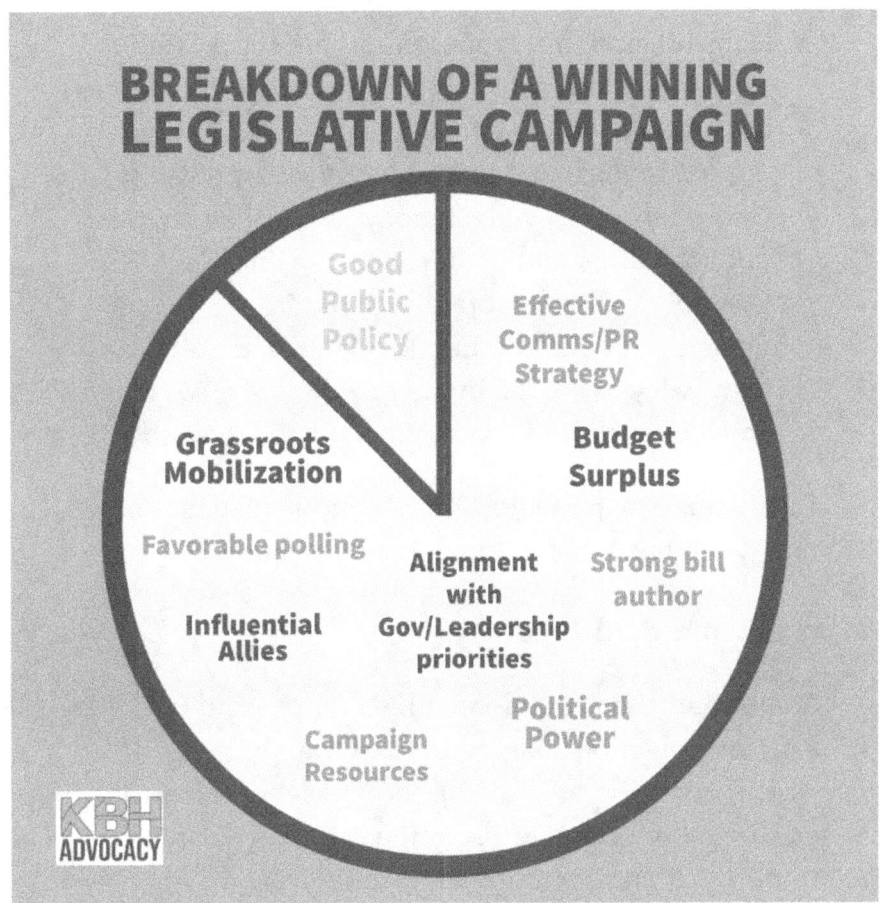

Image credit: KBH Advocacy

Too many advocacy groups focus solely on the merits of their proposal, ignoring other essential factors such as 👆

- Do you have enough resources, i.e., people and funding, to run a campaign for 9 to 12 months?
- Can you mobilize strong grassroots support from throughout the state? This means can you organize lots of Californians to make phone calls or send letters, request and attend lobby visits, travel to Sacramento to give testimony, share their story publicly, and more on behalf of the bill?
- Can you deploy a professional digital communications and public relations strategy?
- How will you build a broad coalition of allies who will actively work with you to push the bill forward?

Take time to map out your assets and liabilities. Know that it can take time to build this foundation.

Is this the right time?

Some years are better than others for passing bills. For example, election years tend to be very busy for legislators trying to shore up their base, which means they may be more selective about the bills they vote for. Depending on your issue, an election year may or may not be a good year to introduce your bill.

Perhaps there are current events that dominate the headlines. Legislation is responsive to what's happening in the state at any given time, especially if there's a crisis. Let's say, for example, that you want to pass legislation that helps impacted communities rebuild after a wildfire.

If this is a year when wildfires are raging throughout the state, the Legislature and Governor are likely to be much more receptive to your proposal.

Bottom line: You will need to take a political "temperature check" to anticipate how lawmakers will respond to your bill. This means getting a sense of whether the Governor and legislators are likely to support or oppose your bill or maybe not care too much either way. You can do this by following current events diligently and reaching out to like-minded organizations and other allies for their insight. You can also request meetings with legislative and Administration staff to ask for their feedback.

 Insider Tip: Many California legislators are active on X (formerly known as Twitter). By following their personal accounts, you can read firsthand what issues they care most about and what legislation they prioritize - or oppose.

Is it politically feasible to pass the bill?'

You also have to consider which groups will be your allies and which will fight you tooth and nail. Are your opponents influential and well-resourced? What arguments will they make against your proposal? You need to know all of this early on so you can prepare accordingly.

Has this proposal been tried in the past?

Has your proposal – or some version of it - been introduced before? If so, by who and when? Why did it fail to pass?

It's a natural blind spot to think we are the originators of brilliant bill ideas. But chances are, someone somewhere came up with a similar idea before you. It's important to know this because you'll want to learn why it didn't work in the past. Are there hidden politics at play? Is there a technical problem no one has been able to figure out? Was it just that the timing was bad and now the issue is ripe for passage?

Take the time to do your research. Watch the video archive of past hearings, talk to others who may have been involved, read stories in the press on past efforts. These steps can help you paint a full picture of what happened so you don't repeat the same mistakes.

Chapter 2 Takeaways

- **WHAT'S THE PROBLEM?**

Identify and clearly articulate the problem you are trying to solve with legislation.

- **DO YOUR HOMEWORK:**

If this is such a big problem, why isn't your idea already a law? Research the constitutionality, appropriate level of government, political feasibility, support and opposition, and previous efforts to pass similar legislation.

- **COUNT YOUR ASSETS:**

When you're ready to propose a bill, survey your assets and liabilities. This includes existing and still needed resources, supporters, organizational power, and expected obstacles.

Chapter 3: Building Support for Your Proposal

It takes a lot of people to turn a good idea into a good law. Let's break it down.

Finding an Author for Your Bill

The "author" of your legislation is the legislator who formally introduces the bill. The group that brings the bill idea to the author is known as the "sponsor." Deciding who you want your author to be is an important consideration. Having the "right" author can make all the difference in getting the bill to the Governor's desk. You may want to create a list of potential authors and deliberate carefully.

Ideally, you want to secure an author who is not just supportive of the idea but who will be a real champion for the bill. That means they'll actively lobby their colleagues and the Governor and will stay in communication with you throughout the process. Unfortunately, some legislators will agree to be your author but are supportive in name only. You might hear from their staff every now and then, but ultimately, you're on your own.

Another thing to consider is that once a bill is introduced by a legislator, they (not the sponsor) have the final decision making power for taking amendments (or not) and moving the bill forward (or not).

Here's a list of who you should first consider as your bill author 👆

- Relevant Committee Chairs
- Legislators who represent districts most impacted by your issue
- Legislative Caucus Chairs
- Legislators with expertise and experience in your issue
- Legislative Leadership
- Legislators who represent your district or the district in which your organization is based

The process of securing an author involves much more than sending a couple of emails or scheduling one or two phone calls.

Think of it as an ongoing process that starts by building relationships. To get anything done in Sacramento, you must start talking to your legislators. Remember, they have been elected to serve YOU.

Building Relationships with Potential Champions

Don't wait until you are ready to present your bill to talk to legislators. Start now so that you already have relationships in place when you're ready to move forward.

To start with, figure out which Senator and Assemblymember represents you. Then, reach out to their offices to request a meeting to discuss the issues that are important to you and your community. Introduce yourself and let them know you're a constituent with concerns you'd like to bring to their attention. If you are part of an organization, you can schedule time for legislators to meet with your leadership team.

Get to know which legislators share your passions. For example, suppose you are trying to pass a bill about prison reform. In that case, you want to seek out lawmakers who are passionate about the issue. In addition to being a natural ally, they can deploy their social and political capital to build awareness and support for it. They'll know the right people to talk to about your bill and can even offer valuable advice.

 Insider Tip: Wondering how you can find out what individual lawmakers care about? Here are some ideas:

- **Pay attention to what they talk about on social media and in the press.**
- **Participate in their community events and ask them directly.**
- **Listen to episodes of the Look West podcast, produced by Assembly Democrats, or Then there's California from Senate Democrats.**

With relationships in place, it will be easier to have conversations with potential champions about your bill.

When the time comes for those conversations, you will need to be specific. Some advocates get uncomfortable asking legislators directly for what they want. But if you don't tell them in clear and concise terms what you would like from them, they won't know. And if they don't know, they can't help you.

Remember, legislators are talking to hundreds of people and organizations on a myriad of policy issues all the time. They might field dozens of inquiries each day. They and their staff won't have the time or inclination to read between the lines of your conversation. So, if you're not crystal clear on your request and you don't follow up on it regularly, chances are it will fall through the cracks.

Be confident and straightforward as you make your case. Explain why you want them to champion your bill. Cite earlier work that they have done that you believe makes them the perfect author. The more personal the bill is to a legislator, the more likely they are to take it on.

Building Grassroots Support

Your bill author plays a pivotal role in your legislative campaign. But they aren't the only people who can make a big impact. You also need to build community support for your bill. This can be done in several ways 👉

- Identify organizations with interests that may align with what you're trying to do. Consider groups that represent impacted communities or key stakeholders. If it makes sense, reach out to share your ideas and ask for meaningful feedback. Assess if there's a potential to collaborate now or in the future. This will grow your network of allies, and it will make your bill stronger and your campaign more likely to succeed.

- Start building relationships with local and state journalists who cover stories related to your issue. Send them an email or DM introducing yourself and your organization and perhaps comment on their past articles. Share what you are working on. Offer to be a resource to them for future articles. Once you're comfortable, pitch them a story about your proposed legislation and why it's necessary.

- Identify local influencers who have built trust and visibility in the community. They can be local elected officials, religious leaders, school board members, or other local leaders. Request to meet with them to introduce yourself, your organization, and your proposal.

- Support allied organizations, locally and around the state. Grow your network of allies by participating in coalitions and stepping up to help when called upon. Form partnerships that serve communities beyond yours.

Start building these relationships now so that you have people to call on when the time comes for your bill to be considered.

Chapter 3 Takeaways

- **CHOOSE WISELY:**

Research legislators before you approach them with a request to author your bill. Remember that they have the final say in how to move the bill once it's introduced!

- **START BUILDING RELATIONSHIPS NOW:**

Establish yourself as a reliable partner with allied groups, as a vocal constituent with elected officials, and as a subject matter resource for members of the media.

Chapter 4: The Legislative Process

The process for creating a new law in California is long and painstaking. Let's take it step by step. The graphic on the next page shows an example of how a bill – in this case a fictional Assembly Bill 123 – might successfully pass through the Legislature.

Step 1: A bill is introduced by a legislator in the Assembly or the Senate. The specific house in which it's introduced is referred to as the "house of origin." The first bill introduced in the Assembly is Assembly Bill 1 (AB 1). The 300th bill introduced in the Senate is Senate Bill 300 (SB 300). You get the picture.

Step 2: It is then assigned by the Rules Committee to the relevant policy committee(s). Usually, that's one committee, but depending on the complexity of the bill, it can be referred to two and sometimes even three policy committees! A bill is taken up or "heard" at a hearing of the relevant policy committee and must pass by a majority vote of the committee members to move on to the next step.

Step 3: If your bill has costs associated with it (for example, if it would require the state to pay for its implementation or enforcement), it is then referred to the Appropriations Committee. The job of "Approps" committee is to review the fiscal impact of the bill only.

MOVING THROUGH BOTH HOUSES

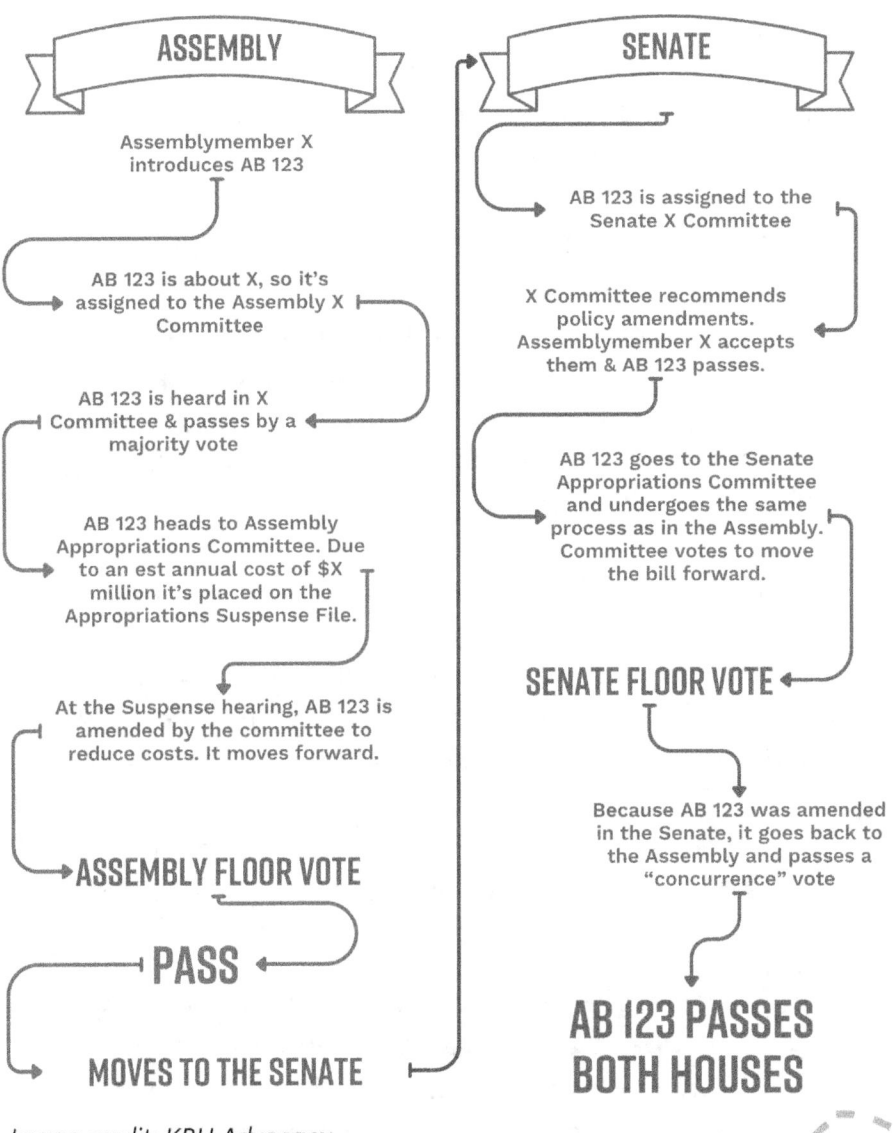

ASSEMBLY

Assemblymember X introduces AB 123

AB 123 is about X, so it's assigned to the Assembly X Committee

AB 123 is heard in X Committee & passes by a majority vote

AB 123 heads to Assembly Appropriations Committee. Due to an est annual cost of $X million it's placed on the Appropriations Suspense File.

At the Suspense hearing, AB 123 is amended by the committee to reduce costs. It moves forward.

ASSEMBLY FLOOR VOTE

PASS

MOVES TO THE SENATE

SENATE

AB 123 is assigned to the Senate X Committee

X Committee recommends policy amendments. Assemblymember X accepts them & AB 123 passes.

AB 123 goes to the Senate Appropriations Committee and undergoes the same process as in the Assembly. Committee votes to move the bill forward.

SENATE FLOOR VOTE

Because AB 123 was amended in the Senate, it goes back to the Assembly and passes a "concurrence" vote

AB 123 PASSES BOTH HOUSES

Image credit: KBH Advocacy

If the committee determines that the bill costs more than a specific dollar threshold (an amount set by each house - usually in the $100,000-$200,000 annual range), it is automatically placed on the committee "suspense file". Because the dollar threshold is so low, most bills are placed "on suspense".

Bills placed on suspense are held there for a period of time until they are all taken up by the committee during a single hearing in late May. The timing of this hearing - after April 15th Tax Day - is intentional. At that point in the year, lawmakers have a more accurate picture of how much state budget revenue is available before making decisions on spending.

At the suspense hearing, the Committee Chair announces the fate of each bill, determined by a committee vote held prior to the hearing. If your bill is "moved off suspense" - congratulations! Your bill passed out of the committee and is now heading for a floor vote.

If your bill is "held in committee" - or not announced at all - this means it has not moved forward. In other words, it "dies".

 Insider Tip: The Suspense file process is largely opaque to advocates. Deliberations happen behind closed doors, which is why advocates find it a mysterious and frustrating exercise. Links to learn more about the Appropriations Suspense File are in the References section.

Step 4: Once the bill passes out of all committees, it goes for a vote of the entire house. This is known as a floor vote. In most cases, it must pass by a simple majority vote to continue. That means you'll need 21 yes or "Aye" votes in the Senate and 41 in the Assembly.

Step 5: If successful, the bill goes to the other or "second house," and the process starts again.

Step 6: It is assigned to the relevant policy and fiscal committees. Again, a bill must pass each committee to move to the next. Keep in mind that a bill can be amended- or changed - at any stage in the committee process, and there is no limit to the number of amendments.

Step 7: The bill is again taken up for a vote on the floor, this time in the second house. After passage, if the bill was amended in the second house, it would then go back to the first house for a "concurrence vote" on the floor. If the bill was amended significantly, it must go back to the policy committee(s) in the first house. This ensures both houses approve the same and final version of the legislation.

Step 8: If successful, the bill is sent to the Governor, who will either sign or veto it. The Governor can also decline to sign or veto a bill, which is unusual but results in the bill becoming law without their signature. Additionally, the Legislature can choose to override a Governor's Veto with a two-thirds vote of each house, however, in California, this is a rare occurrence.

If a bill fails passage in committee or on the floor, the author can request reconsideration, which means they are asking for it to be taken up again for a vote. This request may or may not be granted. Either way, if this too fails, the bill is dead. This means you must start over again the following year.

Of course, this is a highly simplified version of the legislative process. But you can see that trying to pass a bill isn't a quick or easy thing to do. It's not a matter of sending a couple of emails and calling it a day. Advocates must be diligent and involved at each step to ensure the bill has enough votes to move forward.

 Insider tip: In most cases, bills must pass by a majority vote of the membership of the Assembly and the Senate to proceed to the second house. There are certain exceptions, though, when a two-thirds vote is required. This includes urgency bills (bills that take effect immediately upon the Governor's signature), bills that appropriate state dollars, and bills that alter state taxes or fees.

Pay attention to the Legislative Calendar

To successfully navigate the bill-making process, you must follow the California legislative calendar with its numerous deadlines. Why is this important? If your bill doesn't meet a specified deadline, it will die.

You can find the legislative calendar online. It will change from year to year, so make sure you are working with the current version.

In addition to following the annual calendar, check out the California Legislative Information site, known as "Leg Info", to read and track every bill introduced in the current session and in prior years.

Finally, you can track what's going on every day by referring to the "Assembly Daily File"and the "Senate Daily File". Daily Files feature the dates, times, and agendas of committee hearings and floor sessions. You can find links to each in the References section.

 Insider Tip: Legislative deadlines can catch you off guard if you're not paying attention, and the process can move slower than you think. The best way to stay on top of things is to remain in constant communication with the person "staffing" or leading the bill in the author's office.

Chapter 4 Takeaways

- **WHERE IS YOUR BILL?**

The legislative process is complex, with many committee and floor votes. It's important to keep track of which house and committee a bill is in and who will be voting on it next.

- **DEADLINES MATTER:**

Pay attention to the legislative calendar to make sure that you're engaging with the right legislators and staff at the right times of the year and that you don't miss key deadlines for submitting important information.

Chapter 5: Lobbying You Legislation

You've introduced your bill and it's moving through the legislative process. Now the fun part begins.

Reflections: I used to think "lobbying" was a dirty word. Until I started working in Sacramento years ago, I assumed all lobbyists were like the shady political operators you see in the movies and on TV. Over time, I realized that lobbying is not dirty or sleazy in and of itself. It simply means pushing for the policies and investments your community needs and wants.

Sure, there are lobbyists who push for the narrow interests of corporations and the super-rich at the expense of everyone else. But there are also lobbyists who fight to protect families, workers, and the planet. We need these lobbyists more than ever!

Identify Your Priority Legislators

As noted above, your first priority should be to meet with potential bill authors or champions. Your second priority should be to request meetings with the Chair and members of the first policy committee that your bill will need to pass through. Then you can move on to those sitting on the next committee you'll need to pass through, and so on.

By reviewing the list of Senate and Assembly standing committees you can anticipate to which committee(s) you're most likely to be assigned and learn more about them.

Keep in mind that if you're successful enough for your bill to pass through its committees and reach the floor, every lawmaker in that House will vote on your bill. So, in the end, you will want to meet with as many legislators as possible, especially Leadership. But you should prioritize to make sure you see them in the correct order.
Unless you are meeting with Leadership, you may want to hold off on requesting a lobby meeting with a legislator if your bill is not being heard in their committee or house. Legislators are inundated with meeting requests, and many will ask you to come back when your bill is up for their consideration.

You can create a simple spreadsheet to keep track of legislators, meeting requests, and outcomes. Include their name, title, contact information, and assigned staff along with a specific column to note how you think they will vote based on your discussions. This is your vote count, a highly confidential document that lets you and your team know where things stand before a vote is taken.

Your goal is to know – as best you can - how each committee member will vote before the actual hearing. Take it from me, you don't want any "surprise" votes at the hearing. That means confirming – and double confirming - your vote count in advance. If you don't have enough votes, you can work with the author's office to request to move the bill to a future hearing date to give you more time to whip votes.

 Insider Tip: An "AYE" recommendation from legislative staff is NOT a confirmed "AYE" vote. This is a common mistake advocates make that results in incorrect vote counts and disappointment when a bill fails to pass out of committee. Only a legislator themselves can give you a commitment on how they plan to vote - and even that is subject to change.

Request and schedule your meeting

You will need to submit a formal meeting request via email to the Scheduler for each legislator. Fortunately, you can use the Capitol Codex, a free, crowdsourced list of legislators and their staff to find their contact information. The link to the Codex is provided in the References section.

Your email should explain who you are, who you represent, what bill you want to discuss, and who will be in the meeting with you. Make sure to include a link to your support letter and bill fact sheet in the email. Expect your request to take at least a week before receiving a response.

Respect the process

Chances are you'll be asked to meet with a staff member in place of the lawmaker. Though not ideal (this is why relationships are so important), it is perfectly normal.

Deliver your message to staffers as you would to a legislator. Remember, staff have legislators' ears and act as gatekeepers.

Be mindful of everyone's time

Just like you, everyone working at the Capitol is busy. Especially legislators. Be respectful of everyone's time. Don't show up late to meetings, and don't cancel at the last minute.

Connect your issue to the legislator's district

If you can, include constituents of the Legislator in your meetings. Have them speak to issues happening in the district. Remember - All Politics is Local!

Tell a story

Whether you're meeting with a legislator or staff member, be sure to talk about the lived experiences of their constituents before diving deep into facts and figures. For example, instead of launching into a statistical analysis of the local housing crisis, say, "Your constituent Mary is going to lose her house next month if you don't take action." Better yet, ask Mary if she is willing to share her story in the meeting. Research shows people are more likely to remember something if they connect with it emotionally.

Neutralize your opponent's arguments

During your lobby meetings, be upfront about who opposes your bill. Let the legislator or staffer know what they should expect to hear from your opponents. Then explain why they are wrong. This gives you a distinct advantage when legislators go on to meet with the opposition as you've equipped them with information to probe their arguments further.

Make a clear ask

This isn't the time to be shy or coy. As I mentioned, no one has time to read between the lines. After you've shared your stories and made your case, clearly and concisely request what it is you want the lawmaker to do. For example, will you author this legislation? Will you sign on as a co-author? Vote yes in committee? Vote yes on the Floor?

Then wait until you get your answer. If the legislator dodges the question, politely ask again. The key here is respectful persistence. If they tell you they will consider your request, ask when you can follow up directly.

 Insider Tip: Don't lose track of time! At the start of your meeting with a legislator or staffer, confirm how much time they can give you. If you only have 15 minutes, don't spend 14 of them telling your story. Give yourself enough time to make your ask, get their feedback, and respond to questions asked of you.

Schedule a follow-up

Finally, at the end of the meeting, thank everyone for their time and ask when and with whom you should follow up. Take down a phone number or email address, and make sure someone on your team is tasked with the follow up.

Send a thank you note or email

Sending a handwritten note thanking the legislators for meeting with you and, if relevant, supporting your bill is a small detail that can make a big difference. Highlight a key point you discussed, so they remember who you are. Keep it short and sweet. If a handwritten note is not possible, send an email.

Follow up

Stick to the pre-arranged schedule for following up, which you finalized at the end of your conversation. If you don't hear back, follow up again. You may need to follow up many times before you get a commitment. Don't give up! Getting a firm commitment is your goal.

Additional Tips

The steps listed above are for each lobby visit. You'll have a lot of them. It's going to feel exhausting, and you may get sick of repeating yourself over and over again. Remember, though, that your audience is new with every meeting. They don't know the backdrop. They need to see your enthusiasm. Your energy needs to be as high during conversation 100 as it is in your first conversation.

Building Support from the Governor on Your Bill

Last but certainly not least. As you move through the legislative process, don't forget about the Governor! Convincing them to sign your bill is usually (but not always) an advocate's greatest challenge. This means you need to map out your Governor strategy early in the campaign.

In the Governor's Office, there are Deputy Legislative Secretaries, each of whom is assigned to specific issue areas. They serve under the Legislative Secretary, who reports directly to the Governor on all legislation.

When your bill reaches the second house, you should request to meet with the Deputy Secretary responsible for your issue area. You will lobby them similarly to how you lobby the legislators. The difference, of course, is that they represent the Governor and their interests and concerns. They might ask technical questions about the bill but expect them to refrain from commenting in any way that might indicate support for or opposition to it.

Early in the process, you'll also want to request meetings with relevant Agency and Departments heads and their staff to share your legislation, ask for their support, and get their feedback. If you need it, ask for technical assistance on the on the bill.

Public policy is complicated. Your goal is to make sure the bill you send to the Governor's desk is implementable.

Insider Tip: Don't interpret technical assistance from a department or agency as a sign the Governor supports your legislation. Department and agency representatives are not authorized to speak on behalf of the Governor.

If a Constitutional Officer has jurisdiction, ask to meet with them as well to share your proposal and ask for their support. Finally, ask around: who has the Governor's ear on this issue? Who do they listen to? These are also people you want to connect with to share information and ask for support.

A word of caution: The California Political Reform Act requires "Individuals, businesses and other organizations that make or receive payments to influence state governmental decisions – such as advocating for or against legislative bills and state agency regulations – to register as lobbyists and submit periodic reports of their lobbying activity."

I am not a lawyer, and this book does not constitute legal advice. I highly recommend you consult with an expert to determine if you have any obligations under the law. You can start by visiting the website of the Fair Political Practices Commission.

Chapter 5 Takeaways

- **MAP YOUR ROUTE TO SUCCESS IN THE LEGISLATURE:**

Talk to the right legislators at the right times with the right people in the room. Use practiced, effective talking points and follow up frequently!

- **MAKE YOUR CASE TO THE ADMINISTRATION:**

Your bill will almost certainly impact someone or some processes in the Executive branch. Figure out who and what it is and get their assistance and support.

- **FOLLOW LOBBYING RULES:**

Check the FPPC website to make sure you're adhering to lobbying reporting, rules, and requirements when you're advocating for your bill.

Parting Words

And there you have it. Thirteen years of tips and tricks baked into what I hope is an approachable, easy to use guidebook to get you started on the path to policy making success.

A new legislative session is just around the corner. As you gear up for it, I offer you these final words of advice:

- When it comes to advocacy, it's wise to play the long game. Most of the time, the path to success is not quick or linear. Chances are you'll do a lot of backtracking and circling back before you reach your final policy victory. At the Capitol, we like to say policies need time to "marinate". This is normal. Don't get discouraged.

- Your integrity is everything: Resist the temptation to embellish the facts. If you don't know the answer, that's ok. Just be transparent and follow up with the answer. Similarly, don't share confidences meant just for you. Believe me, the Capitol community is small, and word gets around. Relationships are the coin of the realm. And you can't build relationships without trust. I promise it will pay dividends down the road.

And no matter what, you got this. Keep going.

References

2024 Legislative Deadlines. California State Assembly.
https://www.assembly.ca.gov/schedules
publications/legislative-deadlines

Assembly Daily File. California State Assembly.
https://www.assembly.ca.gov/schedules
publications/assembly-daily-file

California Legislative Information.
https://leginfo.legislature.ca.gov/

Capitol Codex: Crowdsourced #CALeg Spreadsheet. Paco Torres.
https://docs.google.com/spreadsheets/d/1gFeGy72R_-
FSFrjXbKCAAvVsvNjyV7t_TUvFoB12vys/edit#gid=1422908451

FAQ's. Senate Appropriations Committee.
https://sapro.senate.ca.gov/FAQs#:~:text=What%20is%20Susp
ense%3F,referral%20to%20the%20Suspense%20File.

Glossary, Office of Legislative Counsel.
https://legislativecounsel.ca.gov/glossary

Graves, Scott. Dollars & Democracy: A Guide to the State Budget
Process. California Budget and Policy Center. Updated December
2021.
https://calbudgetcenter.org/app/uploads/2021/12/State
Budget-Process-Guide-Dec-2021-Final-.pdf

Legislative process. California State Assembly.
https://www.assembly.ca.gov/legislativeprocess

Lobbyist Rules. California Fair Political Practices Commission.
https://www.fppc.ca.gov/learn/lobbyist-rules.html

Look West: How California is Leading the Nation Podcast.
California Assembly Democrats.
https://asmdc.org/look-west

References continued

My Reps. DataMade and Participatory Budgeting Project.
https://myreps.datamade.us/index.html

Nicole Nixon. Understanding how a California bill dies without public debate. Capitol Public Radio. May 16, 2023.
https://www.capradio.org/articles/2023/05/16/understanding - how-a-california-bill-dies-without-public-debate/

Org Chart. Office of Governor Gavin Newsom.
https://www.gov.ca.gov/orgchart/

Rosenhall, Laurel. The suspense files: California bills vanish almost without a Trace. CalMatters. June 23, 2020.
https://calmatters.org/politics/2017/09/capitol-suspense california-bills-vanish-almost-without-trace/

Senate Daily File. California State Senate.
https://www.senate.ca.gov/dailyfile

The Budget Process: A Citizen's Guide to Participation. California State Senate.
https://www.senate.ca.gov/sites/senate.ca.gov/files/budget_process_guide.pdf

Then There's California Podcast. California State Senate Democratic Caucus. https://thentherescalifornia.libsyn.com/

About the Author

Kristina Bas Hamilton is a contract lobbyist and political consultant based in Sacramento, California. She is the founder and CEO of bespoke consulting firm KBH Advocacy, advising progressive advocacy and labor organizations throughout California. She is also the producer and host of the award-winning podcast Blueprint for California Advocates.

Kristina was raised in New Jersey and is a proud daughter of blue-collar immigrants. She earned a bachelor's degree in political science and a Master of Labor and Industrial Relations degree from Rutgers University. She's worked in the house of Labor for over twenty years, from her first job as a research assistant for the faculty union at Rutgers University, to serving as a research analyst for AFSCME District Council 37 in New York City and representing state workers at CWA Local 1034 in Trenton, NJ.

From 2010 through 2020, Kristina had the privilege of representing homecare workers employed through California's In-Home Supportive Services (IHSS) program. She served as Legislative Director for the United Domestic Workers (UDW/AFSCME Local 3930), representing 120,000 IHSS and 20,000 family childcare providers in 45 counties.

In 2014, Kristina led efforts to pass SB 855, historic legislation that extended the right to overtime pay to over 400,000 IHSS workers. This resulted in a $300 million annual and ongoing increase in worker pay.

Kristina is a recognized expert on the direct care workforce. In 2019, she was appointed to Governor Newsom's Master Plan for Aging Stakeholder Advisory Committee. In that same year, she was accepted into the National Academy of Social Insurance (NASI).

Kristina is married to her best friend, James, and is mom to two school-age children and Zuko, the wonder dog.

To learn more about Kristina Bas Hamilton at https://www.linkedin.com/in/kbashamilton/. To learn more about KBH Advocacy visit https://www.kbhadvocacy.com.

www.ingramcontent.com/pod-product-compliance
Lightning Source LLC
Chambersburg PA
CBHW070747310526
45791CB00029B/2060